YO-BEJ-969

MEMPHIS
VISIONS

Created for The Chamber

by the TOWERY Group

Art Director: Brian Groppe

Editor: David Tankersley

Copyright © 1988 by Towery Publishing, Inc.
All rights reserved, including the right to reproduce this work in
any form whatsoever without permission in writing from the
publisher, except for brief passages in connection with a review.
For information, write:

The Donning Company/Publishers
5659 Virginia Beach Boulevard
Norfolk, Virginia 23502

Library of Congress Cataloging-in-Publication Data

Memphis visions/by the Towery group.
    p.   cm.
    ISBN 0-89865-738-5 (lim. ed.)
    1. Memphis (Tenn.)—Description—Views. I. Towery
Publishing. Inc.
F444.M543M46   1988
976.8'19—dc 19   88-23713
                                                    CIP

Printed in the United States of America

THE
DONNING COMPANY
PUBLISHERS
NORFOLK/VIRGINIA BEACH

The Chamber
Memphis Area Chamber of Commerce

BEN FINK

Memphis Visions attempts to reflect the personality of Memphis. Simply put, such an attempt is not very simple. Memphis has a personality of fantastic dimension. It is imbued with the heritage of a river, of music, of cotton, of business and industry, medicine, and hundreds of thousands of people who live and work here.

Memphis' life is far too grand to be "captured" by any pictorial presentation by any group of photographers. The point of this book is not to capture a city. Rather, it is to share personal glimpses into our community. There will be at least one special place or event you will miss being in the book. But, ours is a big city, with too many special scenes, too many people, too many events, and just too much life to have it all slipped into 160 pages. (We'll do another book later on if you like this one enough.)

Memphis Visions does not present Memphis in the "safe" manner that so many city pictorial books have done. You can look at other city pictorials and with few exceptions, a name change would be the real difference among them. We wanted to produce a book representative of as many views of the city as possible. We wanted beautiful homes, parks, churches, and gardens to be included, but more importantly, we wanted scenes of everyday life, of our neighbors and neighborhoods, of those views of life and living and work and play that represent the real Memphis.

So, our selection of photographs requires you to examine them as both symbols and reality. They are symbols of real events, real people, and real places.

The works of some twenty-five photographers went into the creation of this book. A special "thank you" to those photographers who participated with their imagination and skill. Thousands of shots were examined and studied in the attempt to capture a true reflection of Memphis. There were at least an equal number of photographic insights and photographers that were not used.

The Memphis Area Chamber of Commerce takes special pride in its sponsorship of *Memphis Visions*. It represents our vision of Memphis. We know that business and commerce are the lifeblood of the city. And, we know that Memphis is people. It is, after all, the individuals who call Memphis home and their daily lives that create the real city. So, this book is dedicated to you, the people of Memphis.

Memphis Visions can serve as more than just another pretty picture book for your personal library or living room coffee table. We hope you will examine each photograph as if it were being shot, right now, before your own eyes. Maybe, it will help you see more vividly what you see everyday as you work and play and live here.

Finally, we hope *Memphis Visions* provides you an opportunity to take another look, a closer look, at your Memphis and causes you to take even more pride in a growing and maturing city.

David W. Cooley
President,
Memphis Area
Chamber of Commerce

An afternoon sun reflects off the Morgan Keegan Building.

Next pages Court Square at night.

JACK KENNER

JACK KENNER

ALAN PEELER

PHYLISS SMITH

Above   Clock in front of Memphis College of Art at Overton Park.

Left   Softly focused flowers at Dixon Gallery and Gardens.

Opposite   Azaleas and statuary at Brooks Memorial Art Gallery.

First Tennessee Bank.

WALTAIRE BALDWIN

GARY WALPOLE

Baptist Memorial Hospital.

Holiday Corporation's
Executive Center.

JACK KENNER

The Crescent Center office
complex in East Memphis.

ALAN PEELER

WILLIAM E. BARKSDALE

Delta farmland flashes with a summer storm.

Opposite Herman "Alabama" Alexander brings the musical heritage of Beale Street to life, at the feet of W. C. Handy.

PAUL DAGYS

WILLIAM E. BARKSDALE

PAUL DAGYS

Top Cotton picking.

Above left The Cotton Exchange reflects a tradition of cotton trading and the city's heritage as the nation's center of cotton spot-buying.

Phil Johnson, cotton broker, uses computer-assisted marketing and instant trading capabilities.

Opposite Billy Dunavant, President of Dunavant Enterprises, stands in a cotton classing room, where cotton is inspected and rated.

A lone golfer at Galloway Golf Course strolls under a double rainbow.

PAUL DAGYS

Dow-Corning Wright. Pouring chromed cobalt into hip-implant molds.

JACK KENNER

Opposite Sunlight glows from Weil Brothers Cotton Building downtown.

STEVE DAVIS

Above Afternoon on the Mid-America Mall. Officer L.K. Edwards introduces his shy, equine partner to an inquisitive Artwynn Phillips.

Right The carousel at Libertyland.

STEVE DAVIS

WILLIAM E. BARKSDALE

Reminiscent of the pilot house days of Mark Twain, a towboat captain directs barges filled with Midwestern grain down the Mississippi River.

JACK KENNER

Excursion boats docked on
the Mississippi River, as the
channel reflects lights from
Mud Island.

PHYLISS SMITH

Above A late afternoon sun silhouettes a carriage at Main and Beale.

Rounding the bend.

PAUL DAGYS

JACK KENNER

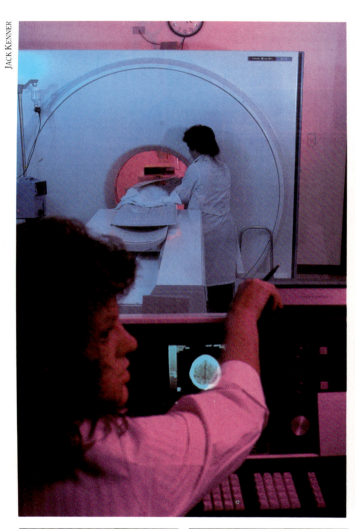

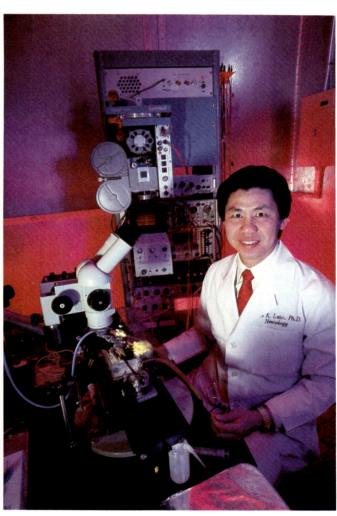

JACK KENNER

Opposite Data Communications Corporation. DCC is a leader in communications market research.

St. Joseph Hospital technicians begin a CAT scan.

Dr. Peter Law of the University of Tennessee, Memphis.

JACK KENNER

JANET HAIRE

The courthouse steps provided an ideal setting for a young couple's marriage ceremony. And then there were the photographs.

JACK KENNER

A very close family of giraffes
at the Overton Park Zoo.

JIM HILLARD

Opposite Fans, as in fanatics, pack the Liberty Bowl Memorial Stadium for a pro football game.

Liberty Bowl Memorial Stadium. Capacity: 65,000.

PAUL DAGYS

STEVE DAVIS

STEVE DAVIS

Top Live entertainment at
Rum Boogie, on Beale Street.

Above Beale Street, Memphis.

PHYLISS SMITH

WALTAIRE BALDWIN

WALTAIRE BALDWIN

JIM STEWART

Night lights.

GARY WALPOLE

Opposite Entertainer Rufus Thomas demonstrates the Funky Chicken with some friends at lunch-time entertainment in Court Square.

Above Vegetable and fruit vendors sell their produce on the Mid-America Mall.

STEVE DAVIS

35

STEVE DAVIS

STEVE DAVIS

Opposite At Dupont, Inc.

Above Industrial storage on Presidents Island.

Following page Soybeans.

Next following page Alarm cocks.

WILLIAM E. BARKSDALE

JACK KENNER

JOHN STUBBLEFIELD

STEVE DAVIS

Left Members of the World's Largest Aerobics Class at the Memphis in May International Festival.

Above Memphis in May's Great River Race gets under way from the confluence of the Wolf and Mississippi, just north of downtown.

The Leisure Brothers, contestants in the Memphis in May Barbecue Contest, relax in their booth. True to their name, they took it easy by ordering out from a commercial barbecue establishment.

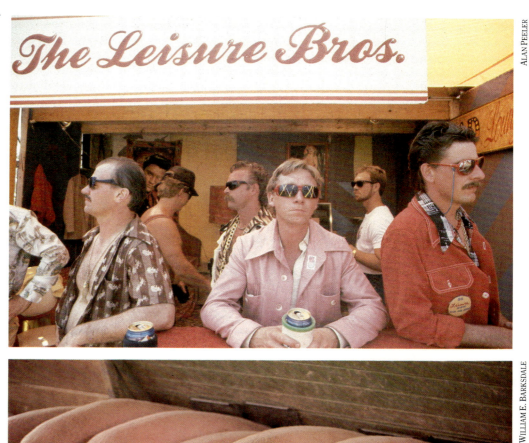

ALAN PEELER

WILLIAM E. BARKSDALE

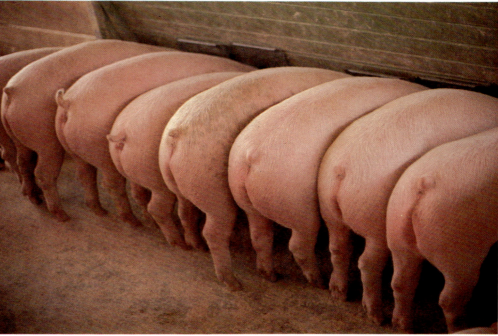

Opposite   Each year, tens of thousands of fun-loving barbecue fans visit the cooking contest at Tom Lee Park on the river. Contestants come from around the world to vie for top honors, and some 50,000 pounds of pork are prepared. Memphis has been called the Pork Barbecue Capital of the World.

STEVE DAVIS

PHYLISS SMITH

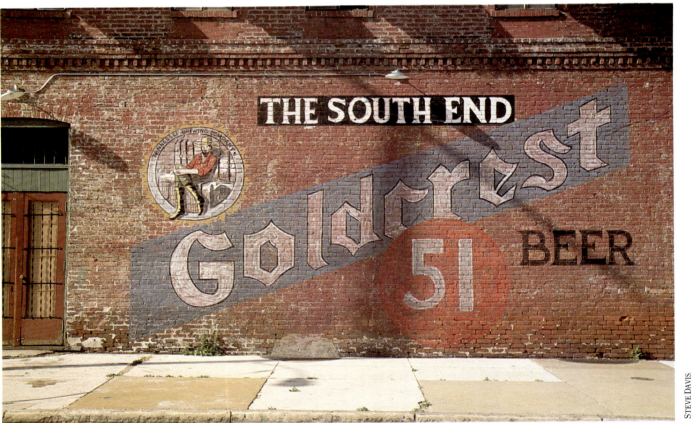

STEVE DAVIS

Top   Architectural detail in
the South Main Street Historical District.

Above   Wall advertisement in
South Main Street district.

BEN FINK

STEVE DAVIS

Top A very big shoe on
Lamar Avenue.

Above Prehistoric wall art in
Midtown.

WILLIAM F. BAWCOM

JACK KENNER

Top An aerial view highlights the city's abundance of trees. The city's downtown skyline can be seen in the distance, at the left of the picture.

Above A speedboat on the Mississippi River.

Opposite Cotton planters sweep Mid-South farmland.

JEANIE UMBRET (DAWSON)

STEVE DAVIS

STEVE DAVIS

Top
"Memphians #4."

Above and right
Tennessee Brewery.

PAUL DAGYS

PAUL DAGYS

PAUL DAGYS

Top Officer Dan Chalk.   Officer Terry Martin.   Officer Dwight Woods.

JANET HAIRE

Opposite   The Hyatt Regency Hotel in East Memphis.

Below   Methodist Hospital technician.

Bottom   St. Francis Hospital.

JACK KENNER

PAUL DAGYS

51

MAC MCMULLEN

MAC MCMULLEN

Opposite and top Federal Express terminal and planes during "the sort." Approximately one million packages can be sorted in one evening and re-loaded to be sent to destinations across the United States and the world.

Above Air traffic controllers at Federal Express manage to launch sixty planes per hour during "rush hours."

BEN FINK

ALAN PEELER

Opposite Interior of Dixon Gallery and Gardens. Dixon features masters of Impressionism and hosts internationally acclaimed traveling exhibits.

Above Guardsmark's corporate art gallery represents one of the largest privately owned collections of Toulouse-Lautrec prints in the world.

Ira A. Lipman, president of Guardsmark, stands in the gallery.

ROBERT JONES

The march of the Peabody Hotel ducks delights guests each and every morning as the feathered family strolls from penthouse to elevator to lobby fountain. In the afternoon, it's back home to the penthouse.

Previous Pages Overton Park, one of the largest inner-city parks in the United States.

JACK KENNER

The Peabody Hotel lobby.

JACK KENNER

PAUL DAGYS

BEN FINK

PAUL DAGYS

Top Sam Phillips, creator of the Sun Sound.

Above Sun Studios, Memphis, the birthplace of rockabilly and Elvis Presley's rock 'n' roll launching pad.

The Presley statue on Beale Street.

PAUL DAGYS

PAUL DAGYS

PAUL DAGYS

Top License plate of the devoted.

Above More than ten years after Elvis Presley's death, fans still come to Graceland to pay their respects to the King of Rock 'n' Roll.

Left The vigil begins on August 16, as thousands gather for the candlelight service on the mansion grounds.

BRIAN GROPPE

A morning's romp is inter-
rupted by a visiting balloon
and a photographer's quick
focus.

ROBERT JONES

At Audubon Park.

Riverside Drive.

JACK KENNER

Opposite
The Hernando DeSoto Bridge.

STEVE DAVIS

PAUL DAGYS

Memphis Polo Association
teams compete on summer
Sundays.

PAUL DAGYS

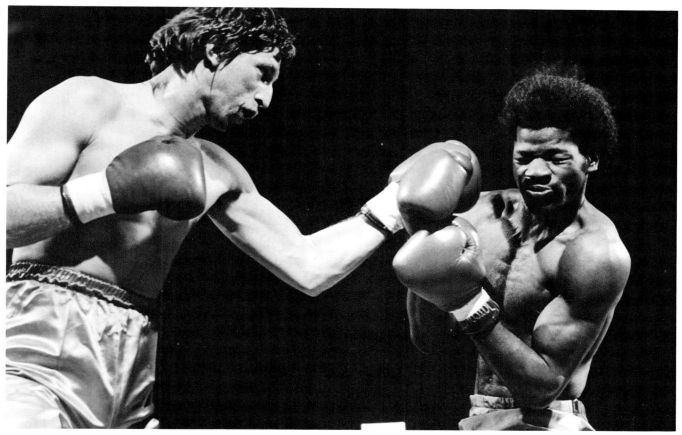

PAUL DAGYS

Above Boxing on Beale Street. Chuck Glover vs. Michael Moss.

PAUL DAGYS

Right Anthony Elmore, the Professional Karate Association's longest reigning super heavyweight champion, works out at his home gym.

The National Blues Award is held each year in Memphis. Photographer Allen Mims' blues-blowing sax captured the spirit of the annual event.

Opposite
B. B. King and The Guitar, Lucille.

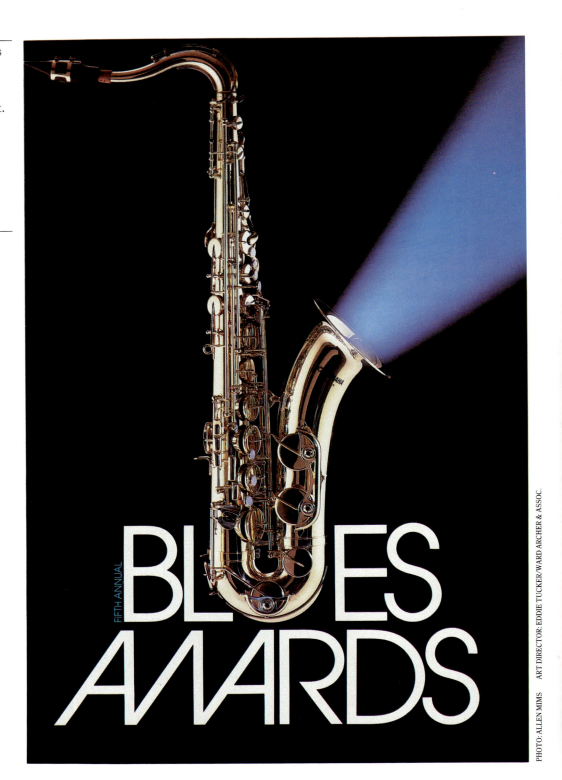

PHOTO: ALLEN MIMS   ART DIRECTOR: EDDIE TUCKER/WARD ARCHER & ASSOC.

PAUL DACUS

JACK KENNER

Dr. Steve Futris of LaGrange, Tennessee, and his '77 Rolls Royce.

ALAN PEELER

A young couple finds an automobile top the perfect place for soaking up the spring sun.

Greyhounds. The dogs run for the money at Southland Greyhound Park in West Memphis, Arkansas.

The Mid-South Fair.

JACK KENNER

73

JACK KENNER

Waitresses at Ferguson's
Restaurant.

JEANIE UMBREIT (DAWSON)

"Memphians #1."

BEN FINK

Night lights at a North
Memphis industrial plant.

Opposite Holiday Inn's
massive communications
network.

JACK KENNER

Alan Peeler

Winter snowstorm on
Memphis State University's
south campus.

Sculpture at the Holiday
Corporation's executive offices.

JACK KENNER

It was a lucky day for this hound as three men assisted him from an icy Chickasaw Gardens lake. Using a ladder to extend their reach, the three heroes pulled him to safety.

BEN FINK

Nativity scene at Graceland.

JACK KENNER

The Christmas parade.

BEN FINK

BEN FINK

Above and left The Veteran's Day parade.

BEN FINK

PHYLISS SMITH

Above The Doughboy, in Overton Park.

Right Memorial to the yellow fever victims at Martyrs' Park by the river.

API PHOTOGRAPHERS

PAUL DAGYS

Bankruptcy Court Judge
Bernice Donald. Judge Donald
was the first black female to
become a judge in the state of
Tennessee.

PAUL DAGYS

Reverend Adrian Rogers of
Bellevue Baptist Church. Dr.
Rogers is twice past president
of the Southern Baptist
Convention.

MAC McMULLEN

Elmwood Cemetery. The cemetery is the gravesite for thousands who died during yellow fever epidemics of the nineteenth century.

MAC McMULLEN

Right
Memphis in May 10K runners.

JACK KENNER

Above series An afternoon's gymnastics demonstration caps off the annual German-town Crafts Fair.

PAUL DAGYS

Dove hunting.

WILLIAM E. BARKSDALE

Members of the Society for Creative Anachronism do knightly battle in Audubon Park.

Opposite   Volunteer belles and beaux greet passengers from the *Delta Queen* as it docks at the river's edge.

STEVE DAVIS

BEN FINK

STEVE DAVIS

Above left
Kids.

Above right
East High School vs.
Trezevant High School.

Opposite   Bo Jackson in his
playing days with the Mem-
phis Chicks. The Memphis
Chicks is a minor-league farm
club of the Kansas City
Royals. Memphian Avron
Fogelman is co-owner of the
Royals.

Tennessee Ballet Company, on
stage at the Orpheum Theatre.

PAUL DAGYS

ALAN PEELER

Evening performance of Tennessee Ballet at Dixon Gallery and Gardens, under moonlight.

PAUL DAGYS

API PHOTOGRAPHERS

LARRY KUZNIEWSKI

PAUL DAGYS

Opposite
Christian Brothers College.

Top University of Tennessee
Memphis, The Health Sciences
Center.

Above Rhodes College.

JACK KENNER

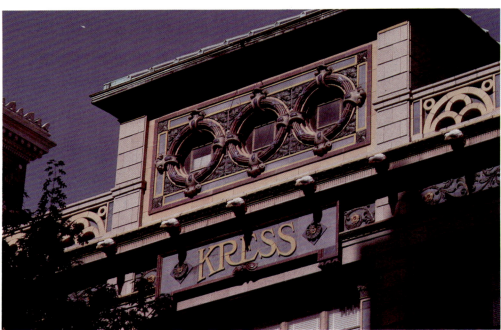

TIM HARPER

JANET HADE

Top Mallory-Neely House in Victorian Village, a collection of nineteenth-century homes located in downtown Memphis.

Above Kress Building on the Mid-America Mall, Main Street.

Opposite The Lincoln American Tower.

STEVE DAVIS

PHYLISS SMITH

Top   Mid-America Mall,
afternoon sax.

Above   Court Square,
Memphis.

Mall Man.

MARK SANDLER

BEN FINK

Above Fashion show at Goldsmith's Department Store.

BEN FINK

Left Rehearsal for Theatre Works' *The Existential Wife.*

BEN FINK

BEN FINK

BEN FINK

Above The Bolshoi Ballet, on stage at the Auditorium.

Top and left Russian fashion show at the Convention Center.

103

GARY WALPOLE

TIM HARPER

Above and opposite Mud Island features the nation's only Mississippi River Museum and provides a microcosmic view of the entire length of the river, from Minnesota to the Gulf of Mexico.

Previous pages The Hernando DeSoto Bridge, the "Bridge of Lights."

TIM HARPER

Taking a break.

JOHN EAKIN

JIM STEWART

STEVE DAVIS

BEN FINK

Above John Martin, known to Memphians as "the guy who waves to you on Walnut Grove Road," and his pooch, Choo Choo.

Top Midtown.

Above Germantown street scene.

JACK KENNER

Hands Across America
reached down Riverside
Drive.

Professional wrestler Jerry "The King" Lawler and ballerina.

ALAN PEELER

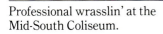

Professional wrasslin' at the Mid-South Coliseum.

BEN FINK

Shriner clowns.

CLAY TOMAS

113

PAUL DAGYS

Opposite James Jackson and Sonia Funches watch an afternoon sunset over the Mississippi River.

Lizzie Walker looks out from the window of her restaurant.

ALAN PEELER

St. Jude Children's Research
Hospital.

LARRY KUZNIEWSKI

JACK KENNER

JACK KENNER

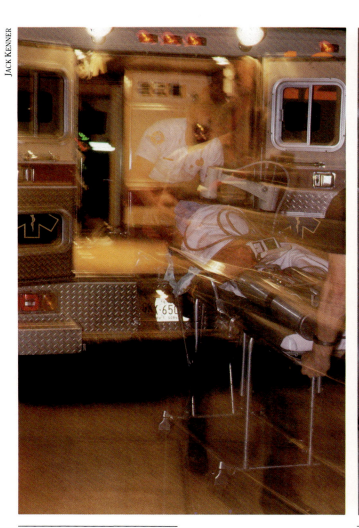

Emergency, Regional Medical
Center at Memphis. The Med.

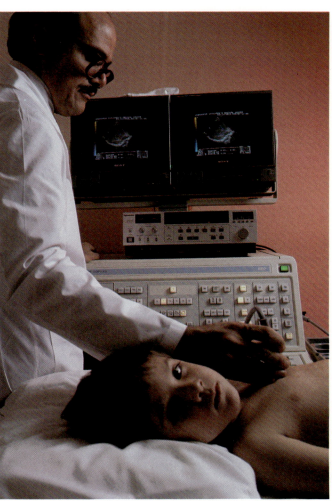

Dr. Thomas G. DiSessa,
LeBonheur Children's Medical
Center cardiologist, using an
electrocardiography machine.

JACK KENNER

PAUL DAGYS

Top
County cows.

Above
Galloway Drive.

Bob Buffalo, collector extraordinaire, sits amidst a small portion of his collection. Buffalo was the first national president of the Cola Clan, an organization dedicated to collecting Coca-Cola memorabilia.

JIM STEWART

Tim Harper

Alan Peeler

Elephant, bear, and flamingoes at the Overton Park Zoo.

JACK KENNER

JANET HAIRE

GARY WALPOLE

Opposite page Airshow spec-
tators at the river bluff.

Top Libertyland.

Above The Revolution ride at
Libertyland.

MURRAY RISS

WILLIAM E. BARKSDALE

BEN FINK

Top Catfish farming.

Above Sign along Monroe Avenue.

Opposite Barges swing down the Mississippi River.

BEN FINK

Tav Falco of the rock group
Panther Burns.

Carriage on Beale Street.

JACK KENNER

CLAY TOMAS

Joseph Sudduth, Jr., photographer at the Peabody Hotel.

CLAY TOMAS

Walter Armstrong, Jr., attorney, bibliophile, and philanthropist, at Rhodes College's Burrow Library. Armstrong donated an extensive collection of rare editions to the school.

JEANIE UMBRETT (DAWSON)

"Memphians #2."

JEANIE UMBREIT (DAWSON)

"Memphians #3."

PETE CEREN

BRIAN GROPPE

Above The grand opening of the exhibit at First Tennessee Bank.

Left In 1979 Ted Faiers was commissioned to create The First Tennessee Heritage Mural for First Tennessee. The individual pieces in the mural combined wood sculpturing and Faiers' unique painting style to capture the essence of Tennessee throughout its history. Faiers died in 1985, and the project was completed by Betty Gillow. The work was displayed publicly in November 1987.

Opposite
Court Square fountain, *Hebe.*

"Alvin York" from Tennessee Centennial by Ted Faiers.

BRIAN GROPPE

Above Alan Balter, maestro of the Memphis Symphony Orchestra, conducts Tchaikovsky's "1812 Overture," a favorite at Memphis in May's beautiful finale, the Sunset Symphony.

Opposite
Sunset.

JACK KENNER

MURRAY RISS

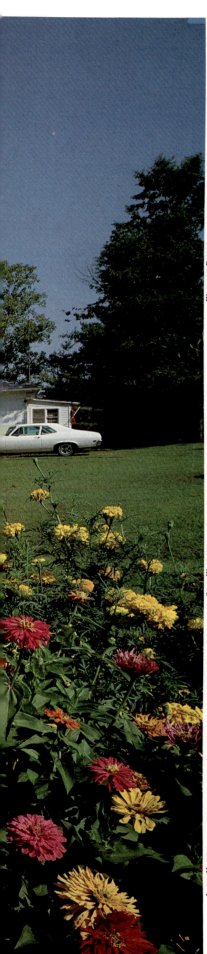

WALTAIRE BALDWIN

A welder puts finishing touches on new office complex.

GARY WALPOLE

Guardsmark Security Officers Charles Chumley, Manager; Eugene Fitchpatrick; and Randall Pierce, Captain, at International Paper's headquarters.

JANET HAIRE

Conveyor at NKC conveyors.

Opposite At work in the flower garden.

137

JIM STEWART

JIM STEWART

Opposite High noon in Court Square.

Youthful Nude at Dixon Gallery and Gardens.

Statue of Edward Hull "Boss" Crump in Overton Park.

BEN FINK

JIM STEWART

BEN FINK

WILLIAM E. BARKSDALE

Opposite A crafts demonstration at Chucalissa Indian Village.

Top Memphis Symphony Orchestra conductor Alan Balter, an accomplished clarinetist, performs for the children at LeBonheur Children's Medical Center.

Above Mississippi Boulevard Christian Church's choir joins the Memphis Symphony Orchestra for a performance of gospel music.

STEVE DAVIS

The Memphis Convention Center.

API

Opposite Southwind features beautiful residences and a professional golf course, home to the Federal Express/St. Jude Memphis Classic pro tournament. The golf course can be seen through the windows of this newly constructed home.

Memphis International Airport.

BEN FINK

BRIAN GROPPE

WILLIAM E. BARKSDALE

WILLIAM E. BARKSDALE

Top Agricenter International's Exposition Center at sunset. The Agricenter features demonstration farming techniques and provides a showcase for agricultural companies and their products.

Above Cotton harvest.

Opposite Soybeans.

WILLIAM E. BARKSDALE

API PHOTOGRAPHERS

Top A crop duster swings low over a field of soybeans.

Above Agricenter lettuce.

Opposite
Tractor, outside of the city.

GARY WALPOLE

The University of Tennessee's satellite link provides extensive teleconferencing capabilities for the world's medical community.

Opposite Goldsmith's Department Store, downtown.

BEN FINK

Jacqueline Smith, the last resident of the Lorraine Motel, takes her message to the street. The Lorraine is the site of the Reverend Martin Luther King, Jr.'s assassination in 1968. It will soon serve as a national civil rights museum.

JACK KENNER

Decadence Manor on Madison Avenue.

JACK KENNER

Opposite   On Beale Street.

BEN FINK

BEN FINK

WALTAIRE BALDWIN

Trucking into Memphis, along Highway 78 in Mississippi.

Bluesman Albert King.

BRIAN GROPPE

Interstate 40, at the Hernando
DeSoto Bridge.

PAUL DAGYS

BRIAN GROPPE

BEN FINK

Top sequence The implosion of the King Cotton Hotel made way for the construction of the Morgan Keegan Office Tower and . . .

Above sequence . . . Arman's sculpture *Ascent of the Blues* and Morgan Keegan.

Opposite The Morgan Keegan Tower, downtown.

JACK KENNER

A jovial group of riverboat
passengers wave to helicopter-
ing photographer Jack Kenner.

Opposite
River silhouettes.

PHYLISS SMITH

Clay Tomas specializes in advertising and editorial work. An early interest in fine art led him to photography as a means of personal expression.

Brian Groppe is a professional designer for The Towery Group. Before returning home to Memphis in 1984, he lived in Berkeley and did design work for several California-based book publishers.

API Photographers, Inc. has been capturing Memphis visually for over 40 years. The company specializes in commercial and advertising work, and also does extensive work in both film and video.

Steve Davis is a commercial and advertising photographer who specializes in brochure work and photojournalism. He prides himself on an extensive backfile of Memphis subjects and scenes.

Janet Haire, a commercial photographer, teaches part-time at the Memphis College of Art. Shooting on a freelance basis since 1985, Haire is a partner in Ceren/Haire Photographers.

Waltaire Baldwin is a photographer/writer from Houston, Texas, now living in Memphis.

Jack Kenner is a nationally recognized photographer, specializing in advertising and corporate work. Kenner's work ranges from fine art to commercial, both on location and in studio. His work has appeared in *TIME* magazine and in *USA Today,* and his stock images are available through both Kenner's studio and The Image Bank in New York City.

Larry Kuzniewski has been photographing Memphis since 1974. Specializing in commercial and advertising work, Kuzniewski has been shooting for *Memphis Magazine* since its first issue in 1976.

William E. Barksdale is an independent agricultural journalist-photographer. He lives in Memphis and works throughout the United States.

Jeanie Umbreit (Dawson) is a fine art photographer living in Memphis. She is currently working primarily in hand-colored silver prints.

Mark Sandler was a professional photographer for over ten years. While he still enjoys personal photographic work, he is employed as a computer programmer for Memphis State University.

Phyliss Smith has been a secretary for the Photo Services Department of Memphis State University for nineteen years. She shoots for personal enjoyment and likes the "out of the way" places.

Alan Peeler, a native Memphian, returned to the city in 1985 from San Antonio, Texas, where he operated a photographic studio. He specializes in fine art and commercial photography, including fashion, architecture, landscape and corporate work.

Murray Riss is an advertising and commercial photographer with a studio on South Main. Riss taught at the Memphis College of Art for several years. His work is displayed in a number of American and foreign museums of art.

Gary Walpole has been involved in photography for over 20 years, and specializes in commercial work. He has worked throughout the United States and in Europe. He does extensive corporate photography.

Tim Harper was a professional photographic printer for several years, before beginning to shoot professionally. He specializes in photo-illustration and table-top photography.

Ben Fink is a professional commercial and advertising photographer who also places great emphasis on personal photography. Fink particularly enjoys the spontaneity of documentary photojournalism.

Pete Ceren, originally from Chicago, has been shooting professionally in Memphis since 1972, and specializes in advertising and commercial photography. He teaches advanced photography classes at the Memphis College of Art.

Allen Mims has been shooting professionally for eight years. He attended Brooks Institute in Santa Barbara, California, and specializes in commercial and advertising work.

John Stubblefield has made a living as a photographer since 1975, specializing in corporate work with an emphasis on medical photography. He is now employed as a photographer for Memphis Light, Gas and Water Division.

Mac McMullen is a corporate photographer for Federal Express, and has been shooting professionally for 13 years. He is experienced in fine art, medical, graphic, and illustrative photography. He is a native Memphian.

Paul Dagys is a Memphis photojournalist who specializes in photographing people in their natural habitat. His clients include *TIME, Forbes, U.S. News, Sports Illustrated,* Federal Express and Holiday Inns.

Robert Jones is well known for his photographic documentation of the South and Southerners. Jones is involved in commercial and advertising work as well as photojournalism. He works extensively with the Center for Southern Folklore.

Jim Stewart has been a studio and location photographer for 10 years, specializing in aviation, architectural interiors and exteriors, and national product advertisements. His clients have included The Boeing Corporation, Design Alternatives, Inc., Exxon Corporation, Federal Express, Hampton Inns, and Signature Suites.

John Eakin is a former student of the Memphis College of Art and Memphis State University, where he concentrated in historical documentary photography. He is presently employed in the Communication Department of St. Jude Children's Research Hospital.

Jim Hilliard is a commercial photographer. He specializes in aerial photography.

STEVE DAVIS

ROSSER FABRAP INTERNATIONAL

PAINTING BY RICK ALLEY

With precise visions of what the city represents today and what it has represented through the years, Memphis continues to focus on a promising and brilliant future.

Top left   Chucalissa Indian Village.

Top right   The model of the proposed downtown Pyramid Arena.

Above   Painting by Commercial Appeal staff artist Rick Alley of Shelby County Mayor William Morris and Dick Hackett, Mayor of Memphis.